You Are So Brave:

Ellie and Leo Go to the Doctor

Written by Anne Kim, Ioana
Moldovan & Karen Jacobs
Illustrations by Joyce Hu

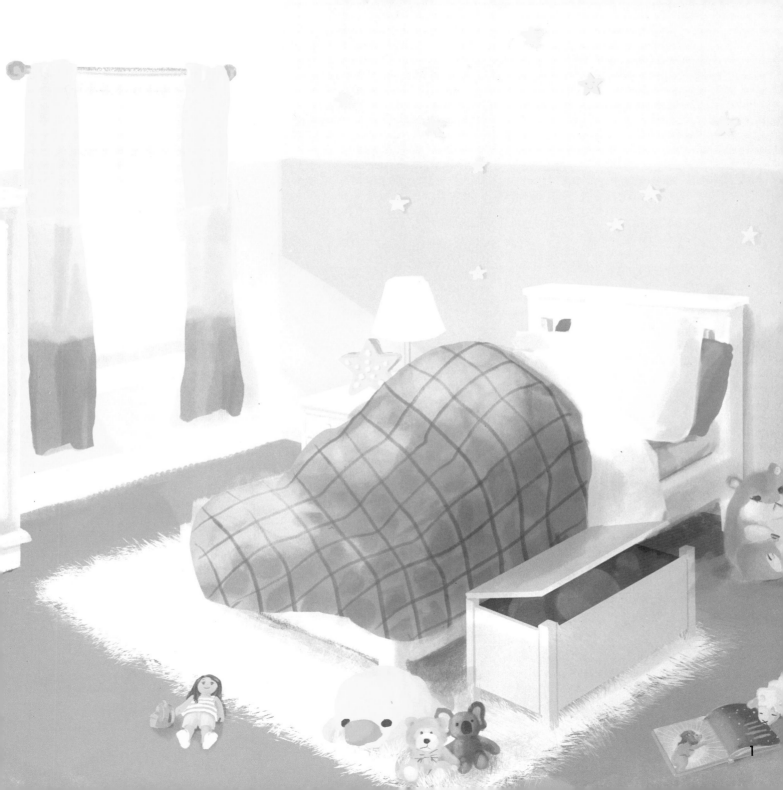

Leo, I have some bad news.
We are going to the doctor
for our yearly check up.

2

Leo, what if I need a shot?
Then you would need one, too.

Don't be scared.
We'll be together.

Ellie, it's time to get dressed!
We don't want to be late for
your appointment!

That day...

8

Sweetheart, it will be okay. Let's take three deep breaths together. Breathe in through your nose and out through your mouth!

We relax our bodies and calm our hearts.

10

We are grateful for our doctor's love and care.

We are happy to be here together.

12

Nurse Kind will first check your temperature.

16

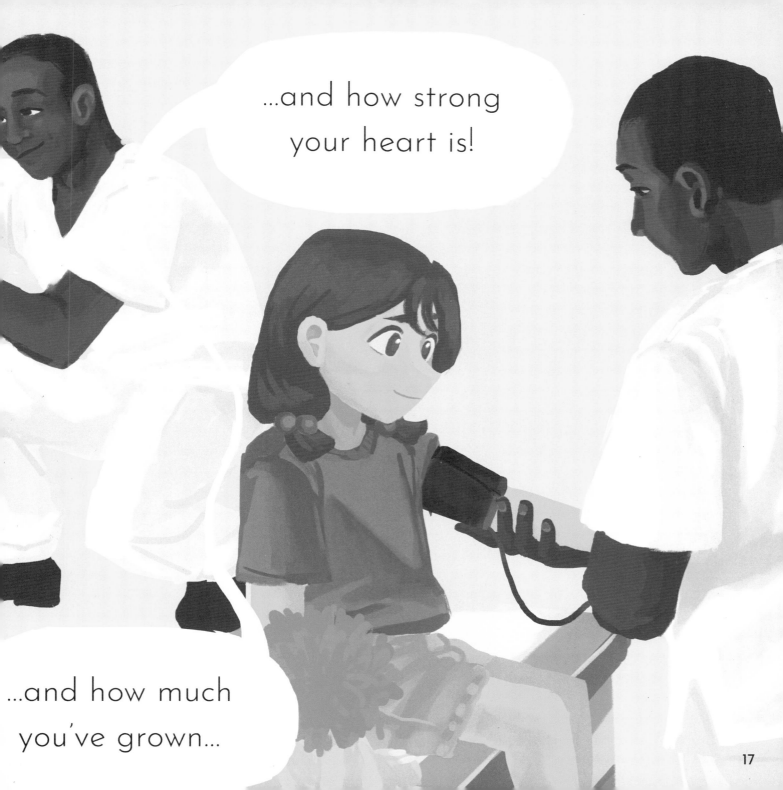

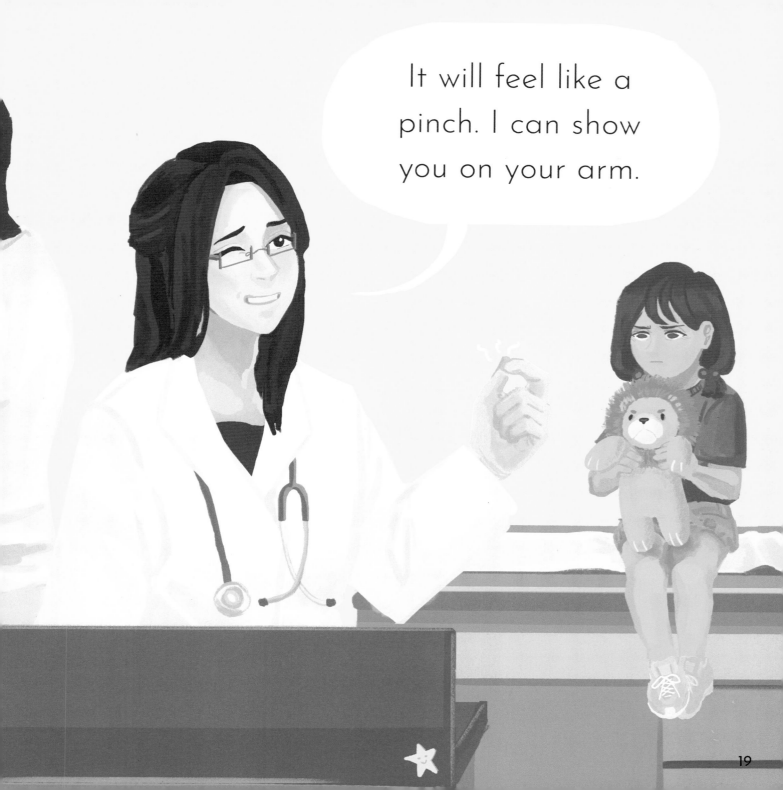

19

21

The real shot will hurt less when you're calm. Remember when you were scared of the dark? We counted the stars in your bedroom with our breaths.

Let's count these stars with your breaths,
and the doctor will give the shot.

All done. **You are so brave!**

That was quick! I thought it was going to be really painful. It didn't hurt too much. It's your turn, Leo.

Discussion Questions

1. Why is Ellie scared of the doctor?
2. What makes Ellie feel brave?
3. When do you feel brave?
4. What did you learn from this book?
5. Did you find the 23 smiling stars hidden in the story?

About Us

ANNE KIM is an aspiring healthcare professional who hugged her favorite toy when she was at the doctor. She studied human physiology and public health while in Sargent College of Health and Rehabilitation Sciences and Kilachand Honors College at Boston University. Using her creativity, Anne enjoyed bringing Ellie and Leo's story to life. She has a passion for photography and hopes to integrate her love for art with medicine in the future. Anne can be contacted at akim1@bu.edu

IOANA MOLDOVAN was scared of shots when she was younger, and now she likes to encourage kids to be brave all the time. At Boston University, she was part of the living and learning community of the Kilachand Honors College as she studied biology and Spanish in the College of Arts and Sciences. She is most interested in exploring the intersection of medicine and the social determinants of health as a future healthcare professional. Ioana may be reached at ioanam@bu.edu

JOYCE HU is an artist at heart studying graphic design and computer science in the College of Fine Arts and the College of Arts and Sciences at Boston University. In the future, she hopes to use both programming and illustration to provide entertainment to people of all ages. She hopes that her drawings will be cherished and that kids reading this story will be comforted by Ellie's journey. Joyce can be reached at joycehu@bu.edu

KAREN JACOBS is an occupational therapist, an ergonomist and a Clinical Professor in the Department of Occupational Therapy at Boston University. Karen is an Amma (grandma in Icelandic) who loves to read children's books to her four grandchildren. Our beloved Ellie and Leo join the family of characters in Karen's 17 other co-authored children's books such as *Breakfast with Grandma Ruthie* and *Charlie's Sensational First Day*. Karen can be reached at kjacobs@bu.edu

Thank You

To our families, friends, and supporters who guided our authorship journey, especially those at Boston University Kilachand Honors College.

CPSIA information can be obtained
at www.ICGtesting.com
Printed in the USA
LVRC012242110919
630747LV00001B/2